A Child's Paradise of Saints

A Child's Paradise of Saints

by Nun Nectaria McLees

illustrated by Elena Stefarova

Christ the Saviour Brotherhood
Indianapolis, Indiana
2000

Printed in the United States of America
Third printing, November 2004

Address all correspondence to:
Christ the Saviour Brotherhood Publishing
PO Box 265
Ash Grove, Missouri 65604
417.751.3183
csbpub@sbcglobal.net

Library of Congress Catalog Card Number 99-80074
ISBN 0-916700-52-6

Contents

*For all Christian children
and those who love them.*

Saints Constantine and Helen

Did you know that Saint Constantine was the very first Christian king? He was the son of a general and later he became the commander of the Roman army. One night, when Constantine was preparing for battle, he had a dream in which he saw a cross shining brilliantly in the dark sky, and he heard a heavenly voice say, "In this sign, conquer!" The next day he went into battle bearing the Christian cross on his standard, and after a long hard fight he defeated his enemies and became the Roman Emperor. He understood that he had won the battle because the Lord Jesus Christ had helped him, and so he became a Christian. Emperor Constantine changed the laws so that Christians could worship without being sent to prison or eaten by lions, and later he built a whole Christian city named Constantinople. Constantinople was full of churches and crosses, and neither pagan temples nor idols were allowed there.

When she was seventy years old, Emperor Constantine's mother, Saint Helen, went to the Holy Land. Her son sent along skilled workmen and much gold to buy precious wood and wonderful marble, so that Saint Helen could build churches at the places where our Lord Jesus Christ had lived and taught when He was on earth. The church in Bethlehem, which St. Helen and her friends built over the cave where the Lord was born, is called the Church of the Nativity, and you can still see it today. The Church of the Holy Sepulchre, on the place where the Lord was crucified, buried and rose from the dead, was more difficult to build. The Romans had destroyed Jerusalem many years before and the holy places were covered with piles of rubble. Almost no one knew where they were. But with heavenly guidance St. Helen found both the Holy Sepulchre and the Cross on which the Lord was crucified.

When St. Helen and her friends found the True Cross, they found not one but three crosses. (You remember, don't you, that the Lord was crucified between two thieves, one on the right and one on the left?) Well, Saint Helen found all three crosses, and didn't know which one had been the Lord's and which had belonged to the thieves, so she prayed to God to show her. As she was praying, a funeral procession came by taking a dead man to be buried. Saint Helen knew that the True Cross wasn't just ordinary wood—it had held the Son of God Himself—so she had the Christians touch the dead man with each of the three crosses. When the Cross of the Lord touched him, he began to stir as if he was waking from a deep sleep and came back to life! God allowed this to happen so that everyone would see the power of the Cross.

Orthodox Christians know that the Cross is very powerful. In fact, next to Holy Communion, it is the most powerful thing in the world, because after the Lord was crucified on it He rose from the dead and opened the gates of heaven for us. Everyone who is baptized, even tiny babies, wear a cross. Before we eat, we make the Sign of the Cross over our food, asking God to bless it. When we need to know an answer (like Saint Helen) or want God to help us, or if we want to thank Him for the help He has already given us, we make the Sign of the Cross over ourselves, so that we pray not only with our minds, and hearts, and mouths, but with our whole body. Every part of us prays.

There is a wonderful song about the Cross that we sing in church. Do you know it?

> The Cross is the guardian of the whole world.
> The Cross is the beauty of the Church.
> The Cross is the might of kings,
> The Cross, angel's glory,
> And wound to demons!

Most of our children know how to make the Sign of the Cross, but if you don't I will tell you now. First, pinch the ends of your thumb and the two big fingers on your right hand together. Place your ring finger and baby finger (the ones left over) in the palm of your hand as if they were bowing, and touch your pinched fingers

Saints Constantine and Helen

first to your forehead, then down to your waist, and finally to your right shoulder and then your left shoulder while saying:

In the name of the Father, and of the Son, and of the Holy Spirit. Amen

The three fingers that are pinched together remind us that there is One God in three Persons, Father, Son and Holy Spirit. The two little fingers lying in the palm tell us that Lord Jesus Christ was both human and divine. So, just think, no matter how little you are, you have all the important things that Christians believe about God, the saints and angels, and all of heaven and earth in your own hand!

In the picture you can see Saint Constantine and Saint Helen holding the True Cross. The little gold cross high in the corner is the one Saint Constantine saw in his dream, and behind him in the background, you can see a smaller picture of him leading his army into battle. The little buildings behind Saint Helen's skirt are the city of Jerusalem, where she found the True Cross.

Holy Saints Constantine and Helen, pray to God for us!

Saints Cyprian and Justina

This is a really amazing story—and it's true. Saint Cyprian was a bishop a very long time ago, but before he was a saint, he was a very wicked man. He didn't do just small things like telling lies to keep from getting into trouble, or talking back; he was much worse than that. You see, Cyprian was a sorcerer—which is a person who uses help from the devil to get what he wants. It wasn't entirely his fault, because when he was young his parents had allowed him to be trained by evil magicians and he had never learned about Christianity. But even so, he was bad, and not just bad like people who are ignorant or weak. Cyprian wanted to be evil, and the harder he studied magic, the worse he got. Not only could he make it rain when it should have been sunny, or not rain when people needed water, but he spoiled the crops and cast spells on people he didn't like so that they would become ill and die.

This kind of magic is different than the heavenly power the Saints have. They don't want things for themselves, because they already have the best thing—heaven. And they don't cast spells. They pray and ask God to help us if it is His will, because only God always knows if something is right for us or not. But Cyprian didn't care about right and wrong—he just did as he pleased. Everyone knows that you can't ask God to help you if you have that kind of attitude, so he asked the devil. The devil is always glad to see good people hurt, or sad, or sick, and he thought that once Cyprian became his servant, he could make him a prince of hell, like himself.

After Cyprian had been a sorcerer for many years, a rich young man named Aglaias came and told him that there was a beautiful Christian girl named Justina whom he wanted for his wife, but that she wouldn't marry him. Aglaias didn't really love Justina; he only wanted to marry her because she was beautiful, and he wanted her beauty for himself. But Justina was no fool; she knew that Aglaias was a scoundrel. More importantly, Justina loved God and wanted to live for Him alone. So when Aglaias asked her to marry him she refused, saying, " My Bridegroom is Christ, Him I serve, and for His sake I preserve my purity...." Aglaias was so angry that he got his friends together and they attacked Justina in the street on her way to church. (You can see what a coward Aglaias was—having to get a whole group of men together to attack one young girl.) Justina was not just any girl, however, and she wasn't weak-spirited. As soon as they seized her she began screaming and beating and spitting. Her neighbors heard her cries and ran to help. They beat Aglaias and his friends off with sticks, and rescued Justina.

Aglaias saw now that he couldn't capture Justina by force, so he went to Cyprian and offered the sorcerer gold and silver if he would use magic to make Justina want to marry him. Cyprian didn't care if Justina wanted to serve God or not, and thought that he could easily overcome a young girl. But he didn't know about Justina's faith, or the Christian God she worshipped.

First, Cyprian sent Justina passionate thoughts and feelings to make her want to marry Aglaias. Cyprian's magic was very powerful, and the demonic thoughts pierced Justina's heart like an arrow. But Justina knew how to do spiritual battle. She made the Sign of the Cross, and kneeling down, prayed for a long time. The Lord heard her prayers and helped her, of course, and by His grace she vanquished the evil thoughts.

Cyprian was very surprised that such a young girl would try to fight against his magic, so he called upon a prince of the demons, who appeared to Justina as an old woman, pretending to be interested in Christianity. The demon began to talk to Justina about how wonderful it would be if she married Aglaias, but when you pray a lot like Justina did, you can easily tell the difference between good and evil. Justina felt in her heart that there was something not quite right with this old woman, so she made the Sign of the Cross, and the demon vanished. (You see, demons cannot bear the Cross, or even being around when someone makes the Sign of the Cross. They feel like they are being burned!)

The demon prince was really angry now, and decided that instead of trying to attack Justina he would disguise himself to look like her, and trick Aglaias into thinking he was the real Justina. However, he didn't know the strength of the heavenly grace that filled the girl. When Aglaias saw the demon-Justina coming to his house, he ran to meet it calling "Justina, Justina!" But the demon prince was so frightened by just hearing the name of the God-protected girl that the false image crumbled to dust.

Next, Cyprian cast a magic spell to turn Aglaias into a big black bird so that he could fly straight into Justina's room. Aglaias couldn't really fly, of course—he had to be carried by an invisible demon. But, just as soon as the demon glimpsed Justina through the window, it vanished in terror and Aglaias fell from the sky. He barely saved himself by catching on to the edge of the roof, and then he hung there, dangling by his hands for everyone to see. He felt just as silly as he looked, and was about to fall when Justina heard his cries for help and rushed to the window. She understood right away what had happened and let Aglaias down gently by her prayers. It takes a really good Christian to be that nice.

Cyprian was furious now. He was the greatest sorcerer in the world and was not about to be beaten by a young girl, so he began casting spells on Justina, her family, the neighbors, and finally, the entire city. He even made the animals sick! The citizens of Antioch knew why the sorcerer was angry, and they came to Justina, demanding that she marry Aglaias so that they would not all perish. Justina felt very sorry and asked them to be patient just a little longer, because she knew that God would soon bring everything to a good end. She prayed hard, and within a short time all the people and animals were healed. Seeing that a weak girl had overcome the sorcerer's spells, the whole city began to glorify the Lord Jesus Christ. They laughed at Cyprian and mocked him until he was so ashamed that he wouldn't even show his face in the street.

When all of his dark spells were exhausted, and Justina was still as immovable as a rock, Cyprian understood that he was defeated. He cursed the prince of darkness whom he had served, and said, "From now on I will follow the Christian God!"

The devil was furious, of course. He didn't want his finest sorcerer to escape, so he summoned a legion of demons to attack him. Cyprian prayed and fasted, and with the Lord's help he drove the evil army away. Then Cyprian went to the Bishop of Antioch and asked to be baptized, but Bishop Anthimos, who knew all about his sorcery, thought, rather sensibly, that this was probably just another trick. Cyprian understood that because he had lied and cheated so often, he couldn't expect to be believed now. So, to show that he really wanted to become a Christian he brought all of his magic books to the Bishop and burnt them in front of him. Then he sprinkled the ashes of the books on his head and threw himself to the ground, begging to enter the Church. The Bishop saw he was truly repenting, and baptized him.

Cyprian struggled for virtue even harder than he had worked at sorcery, and at the end of a year he was so full of grace that he was made a priest. Later he became the Bishop of Nicomedia. He and Justina became friends, and after Cyprian became bishop, he made Justina a deaconess, and put her in charge of a house of virgins, women like her who wanted to give their lives to Christ.

At that time, people were only allowed to worship the false Roman gods. It was against the law to be a Christian. The devil knew this and, because he wanted to destroy Bishop Cyprian, he had evil pagans tell the ruler that Cyprian and Justina were Christians. They were arrested and the ruler ordered his soldiers to scrape Cyprian's body with sharp knives until he bowed down to the idols. Justina was beaten on the eyes and mouth. When they still refused to deny Christ, they were thrown into a boiling cauldron, but they were so protected by God that the steaming water that should have killed them felt like a warm bath. Finally, the ruler ordered that they be beheaded. Justina bravely bent her head under the sword, and in an instant her soul departed to heaven. Then came Cyprian's turn, and he too, endured it courageously, as a martyr of Christ.

All of this happened almost two thousand years ago, but Saints Cyprian and Justina are so powerful that people still pray to them for help against the evil one, and against all forms of magic. They pray to the Lord for us, just as they prayed for

Saints Cyprian and Justina

themselves. Also, it is good to remember that no matter how bad someone is, God can enter their soul and change them, like He changed Saint Cyprian. This is why we must pray for our enemies. Finally, if you ever find yourself afraid or in danger, remember Saint Justina—a young girl who overcame all the dark powers of hell with the help of Our Lord Jesus Christ.

In the picture you can see Saint Justina praying, and that stupid Aglaias trying to come through the window disguised as a bird. In just a moment her prayers will cast out the invisible demon who is helping him fly, and Aglaias will have to catch on to the edge of the roof with his hands, so that he doesn't fall. The other picture shows Saint Cyprian burning the sorcery books. He is already dressed as a bishop, so I think he is burning some other magician's books. After he became a Christian, he helped many people come to Christ, and he still helps today. All you have to do is ask.

Holy Saints Cyprian and Justina, pray to God for us!

Saint Demetrius of Thessalonica

Three hundred years after our Lord walked the earth, there lived in the Greek city of Thessalonica a very brave young soldier named Demetrius. Demetrius was a Christian and because he said that Jesus Christ was the true God, and that he would not bow down to idols, he was stabbed with a sword and died as a martyr. That is how he went to heaven, but it is not the end of the story. Ever since then, Saint Demetrius has been the protector of Thessalonica and its people. For seventeen hundred years he has been helping Christians, and people have seen him even in our own century.

The story that I am about to tell you, however, is not from our time. It is a very old story that goes with the picture you will see when you turn the page. It is called "The Two Maidens."

Once, evil pagans, who did not believe in the true God, but only in lifeless stone idols, came to capture the city of Thessalonica. The Thessalonians were able to ward them off with the help of Saint Demetrius, who appeared from heaven, fighting alongside them on the city walls. When the pagans saw the heavenly warrior's shining and fearful countenance they fled in terror, but they were so angry at having lost the battle that they attacked many little farms and villages in the countryside, taking food and clothes and capturing the people as slaves.

Among their captives were two young Christian women whom they gave as servants to their prince. The girls were both very good at embroidery. (Embroidery is sewing pictures on cloth with a needle and thread, and it is just as difficult as it sounds.) When the prince found out that they could make these cloth pictures, he said, "I have been told that in your land there is a great god named Demetrius, and I want you to make me a likeness of him." The maidens said, "Saint Demetrius is not a god, but a servant of the true God, and the help of all Christians. We cannot make an image of him for a pagan."

The prince became angry and shouted, "If you don't make this picture, I will put you to death!" The girls were very afraid, and sadly began to work on the icon. They finished the embroidery on the eve of Saint Demetrius' Day, and looking at their beautiful icon, they began to weep. One of them wept because they had to spend the feast in slavery, and the other because they had to give the Saint's icon to the prince.

But God saw their tears and heard their prayers, and that very night Saint Demetrius himself appeared on his horse and picked up the maidens and their cloth icon. With angelic speed (which is hardly any time at all), he took them to Thessalonica and set them down in the midst of Saint Demetrius Church. Many Christians were gathered in church for his feast day, and when the girls appeared and told their story, everyone glorified God and His saint.

In the picture you can see Saint Demetrius dressed as a Roman soldier. He has on armor and a soldier's cape, and is carrying a spear. You can always tell an icon of Saint Demetrius because his horse is red. (St. George rides a white horse.) Below him you can see the two maidens escaping from the prince's palace. I'm not sure if they really rode in a leaf-boat, but the artist had to draw it like that so that you would understand that they felt just as safe as anything. The angel was surely there. I don't know if the girls were able to see him, but even if they didn't, he guarded them by the power of God and the prayers of Saint Demetrius.

Holy Saint Demetrius, pray to God for us!

Saint Demetrius of Thessalonica

The Guardian Angel

The Guardian Angel

This is a picture of the Guardian Angel. Surely every young Christian knows that each of us has our own angel, given by God at baptism.

Our guardian angel is always with us, to protect and guide us. When we sin, we turn our back and step away from him, but when we pray to God, struggle to do good, and try to be kind to everyone, he is very close. Do you know how wonderful you feel after you receive Holy Communion? How warm and close to God? Your guardian angel is close to you then too, because this is the time that you are most like him!

Some children have even seen their guardian angel. Have you? I haven't, but once, when I was very little, I prayed to God before I went to bed that I would see a shooting star. I awoke in the middle of the night thinking that someone had just said, "If you get up right now, you'll see a shooting star." I jumped up to look out of the window and, at that very moment, a wonderfully bright star fell through the sky. I knew that it was my guardian angel who had awakened me.

Of course, guardian angels also protect us from danger. I know a fisherman in Alaska whose name is Chris. (That's short for Christopher, the name of one of our great saints.) Once, when Chris was out in his boat, working inside a giant crab trap (which looks like a big cage), an enormous wave smashed against the boat and the trap went over the side with Chris in it! The trap was so heavy that Chris fell straight to the bottom of the ocean. He couldn't breathe, of course, and he was sure he was going to die, but at that very moment his guardian angel appeared and spoke to him. You see, God Himself was watching out for Chris, because another fisherman came up on deck just in time to see him disappear beneath the waves and pulled him up from the ocean floor. Chris's friend was surely helped by angels because it was impossible for him to pull up such a heavy trap by himself. Once I asked Chris what it was like when he saw his angel, but he couldn't tell me. He only smiled and looked at the ground. Some things are just too wonderful to talk about.

Here is another story, about a young Russian woman named Tatiana, and how her angel helped her outsmart some evil people who wanted to send her to prison. Tatiana lived in Russia during the Communist times, which were very difficult for Christians because Communists don't believe in God and don't want other people to believe in Him either. One day Tatiana was arrested and taken to the police station because she was an Orthodox Christian. The police wanted her to say that she didn't believe in God, and she knew that if she said she was a believer she would be sent to prison. Tatiana was very worried, and she prayed hard to her guardian angel to tell her what to say. Suddenly an idea came to her, the voice of the angel in her heart. "Don't answer anything, just keep quiet." When the police began asking questions, she didn't say a word. She just prayed silently and refused to speak. In the end, the police decided that she was a very stupid girl, and let her go free.

Many people also ask their guardian angels for everyday things: to help them pass tests at school, to protect them as they ride in the car or on their bikes, to show them how to get along with difficult people, and how to bring peace to their homes. In Russian homes, when someone leaves for school or work or just to go out to play, people say *"Anghela Kranitela."* That means, "May your angel guard you!"

Remember to thank your guardian angel each night during your prayers, and ask him to help you during the day. The more you pray to him, the more you will feel how close he is. You may not ever see him or hear him speak, but you will know that he is helping you, and sometimes, like Tatiana, you will hear his voice like a good suggestion in your heart. After you die you will meet your angel. It will be like meeting a friend you have known your whole life, and he will take you to heaven.

In this picture, the Guardian Angel is holding a cross and a sword. The cross means that he serves our Lord Jesus Christ the King of the Universe, and the sword means that he is a soldier in God's army. He is always ready to protect us from danger. Whether it is a great danger, like being lost in the woods, or a small one like being afraid to walk down the dark hall to your room, remember to pray to your angel. Some people even ask their angel to bless them so they won't have nightmares. If you are sad or angry, or your feelings are hurt, turn to your guardian angel. He is a great warrior and can help you to vanquish any kind of trouble that arises in your own heart.

When you want your friends to stop fighting, ask your angel to make peace between them. If someone you know is unhappy, ask your angel for the right words to comfort him. Very often children are a little lonely. If you ever feel like this, remember that there is always someone beside you, whom God has given to be your best friend and to watch over you every single moment of the day and night, someone who knows you even better than you know yourself.

Can you guess why the angel is alone in the picture? There are no children or grown-ups or even saints there because this is your own guardian angel. Every baptized Christian has their own angel, and believe me, yours is much more beautiful than the one in the picture.

Holy Angel, my guardian, pray to God for me!

Saint Herman of Alaska

If you are from America or Canada you surely know of Saint Herman. He was a Russian monk, and a missionary to Alaska. Do you know what a missionary is? A missionary is someone who has so much love for God and His saints that he feels he has to share it with other people or he will burst. Some missionaries go to foreign lands, like Saint Herman did. Others stay at home and talk to their neighbors.

Saint Herman came from a wonderful monastery in Russia, called *Valaam*. When he heard that the ruler of Russia was looking for missionaries to go to Alaska to tell the native people about the Lord Jesus Christ, he asked to go. To reach Alaska, he and the other monks had to travel across Russia by horseback. Then they took a small wooden ship over the ocean. Russia is such a large country that the journey took almost a year, and they had many adventures. More than once they were attacked by wild bears that wanted to eat their horses, but, with God's help, they traversed the dense forests and the stormy ocean and arrived safely on Kodiak Island.

In Alaska, Saint Herman was known for his great love for everyone. If anyone was sick or in trouble, he went to help them. Most of the time he lived in the woods on Spruce Island, at a place called New Valaam, where he made a home for orphans—children whose parents had died or who couldn't take care of them. Sometimes people would come to ask him how to be happy. He told them that the way to be truly happy is to love God. *"From this day, from this hour, from this minute, let us strive to love God above all and do His holy will."*

Saint Herman was very strong, which is a good thing for living in the woods. When he built cabins for the children to live in, he often carried whole logs on his shoulder. If you've ever tried to lift even a small log you've found lying in the forest, you'll know how heavy they are.

Saint Herman wasn't a priest, so he couldn't do priestly things like serving the Divine Liturgy or marrying people, but God took care of him anyway. On the Feast of Theophany (the day we celebrate the Lord's baptism in the Jordan River) there was no priest on Spruce Island to bless the waters, so Saint Herman went down to the beach to pray, and an angel came and blessed the waters for him!

Once there was a *tsunami* (an earthquake in the sea) and huge waves began to roll up on the beach at New Valaam, ready to flood the land and wash away the children's houses. Saint Herman took an icon of the Most Holy Mother of God down to the beach, and setting the icon on the shore, began to pray. The stormy waves, which were much higher than his head, came closer and closer. He prayed very hard, and then, suddenly, the flood stopped. The Mother of God had heard his prayers, and when she called on the power of her Son, the waves couldn't go past the icon.

After Saint Herman died, people prayed to him for help and many were healed of illnesses or had their sorrows lifted. Even now, the native people often take earth from his grave as a blessing, especially when they are sick. Many pilgrims who have walked through the woods to his grave at Monk's Lagoon say that the Saint seems so close that they almost expect him to step out from behind a tree. You see, he is watching over the island he loved so much when he was on earth.

Just a few years ago, two young native men, Peter and Herman, came to Spruce Island because they wanted to pray at the place where Saint Herman had lived. Monk's Lagoon is a long way from the village, however, and it is very easy to get lost in the woods. After walking many hours over the moss-covered paths, and picking their way through muddy bogs and the prickly bushes called "Devil's Club," the boys found that they had not come any closer to Monk's Lagoon, but had only walked in a big circle. They were so mixed-up that they couldn't even remember what direction they were supposed to go in.

Suddenly they saw that the sun was setting. It was almost too dark to see, and they began to feel really frightened. But if you think that Peter and Herman were cowards, you are wrong. They were just as brave as you are, and it wasn't the dark they were afraid of. It was BEARS! Spruce Island has very big bears, and Peter and Herman did not want to end up as someone's midnight snack. They were clever boys, though, and so they did the only sensible thing they could do. They knelt down in the forest and asked Saint Herman to help. When they finished praying, they weren't so afraid, because they felt that Saint Herman was telling them they would be all right. They still didn't know where they were going, but they decided to walk with their arms stretched out in front of them so that they wouldn't run into anything in the dark. It was good they did, because after a few moments Peter bumped into something hard, and they found that they had walked right into the back of the little church over Saint Herman's grave!

In the picture you can see Saint Herman with the Aleut children. The black rope in his hand is called a prayer rope, and that is what he counted his Jesus Prayers on. Do you know what the Jesus Prayer is? It is a prayer that many Orthodox Christians try to say all the time: "Lord Jesus Christ, Son of God, have mercy on me!" Some people carry prayer ropes to help them count how many times they say it.

The little chapel and cabin behind Saint Herman are like the ones he built with the logs he carried on his shoulder. I don't know what the names of the boys are, but the little girl on the right is Katherine. You probably didn't know this, but her great-great-great-granddaughter Daria is a young novice in America, and that's another miracle of Saint Herman.

Holy Saint Herman, pray to God for us!

Saint Herman of Alaska

Saint John the Russian

Saint John the Russian

Saint John was a young Russian man who spent many years as a Turkish slave. We don't know what town he was from or his family name, but we do know that he was a soldier in the army of the Russian Tsar, Peter the Great. Tsar Peter had tried to free Constantinople from Turkish Moslem rule, but he lost the battle and many of his soldiers were taken prisoner. Saint John was one of these captives, and he was sold as a slave to a Turkish cavalry officer. To his new master, the Agha, John spoke frankly, "I am a Christian, and if you allow me to practice my religion I will obey all your commands, but if you try to force me to become a Moslem, know that I will give up my head before I give up my faith." He meant that he would rather die than not be a Christian.

John's work was to take care of the Agha's valuable horses, and he was very good at it. His warm heart and his willing service soon made him a favorite of the Agha and his family, and the Agha told his friends that he prospered because he had a servant who was beloved by God. The Agha and his wife wanted to give John a room in their home, but he refused it and slept in the hay loft of the barn instead. He liked the barn because it was warm and quiet and he could pray late into the night. There was a small Orthodox church in the village where he went every week to receive Holy Communion, and even though he was far from Russia, he knew that God was watching over him.

One day, John's master, the Agha, decided to go on a pilgrimage to Mecca, the Moslem holy city. It was a long way, and when he arrived he sent word to his wife, who gave a special dinner for their friends in thanksgiving to God. That night John waited on the table, and the guests had *pilaf* to eat. (Pilaf is a special dish of grain, like rice, with little pieces of meat and vegetables in it.) This was a particularly delicious pilaf, and after she tasted it, the Agha's wife said, "Oh, how I wish that my husband could have some of this!" Hearing her remark, John came to the

Agha's wife and said, "Give me a plate of pilaf for my master." The guests all laughed, thinking that John wanted to eat the pilaf himself, but his mistress wisely granted his request. John took the steaming plate to the stable, and carefully laid it in the straw. Kneeling beside the pilaf, he prayed, "Dear Lord, please take this to my master in Mecca!" At that moment, the plate disappeared right in front of his eyes!

The Agha returned a few weeks later with an equally wonderful story. "When I was in Mecca, I came to my room one evening from the mosque. The door had been locked all day and no one could have entered. When I unlocked the door, I was very surprised to see a plate of hot, steaming pilaf on the table. 'Allah!' I cried. 'Who could have brought this pilaf here when the door was locked?' As I moved closer to the table I was even more amazed—*the dish was one from my own house and had my name engraved on it!* I've brought the dish with me to show you. Tell me! How did this happen?" Those who heard the story were astonished, and they looked in wonder at John, who showed no sign of surprise. The mistress of the house told her husband about John's strange request on the night of the banquet, and the entire household marveled at the man of God.

A few years later John fell ill and peacefully died. The whole village, both Christians and Moslems, honored him as a saint, and the Agha's family prayed to him for generations. There were many miracles after Saint John's death. Through his prayers to the Lord, the sick were healed, the lost were found, and many were saved from danger--but those are other stories, and I will have to tell them to you later.

In the first picture you can see Saint John in the stable, praying that God will take the pilaf to his master in Mecca. Then, on the other side, you see the Agha coming in and finding the hot pilaf. He looks really surprised, don't you think?

Holy Saint John the Russian, pray to God for us!

Saint Mary Magdalene

Do you remember why Saint Mary Magdalene is so important? It is because she is one of the saints who knew our Lord while He was on earth. That is a very wonderful thing in itself, and after His Resurrection she told everyone she met about Him, and many of them became Christians.

Mary was a brave woman. In fact, she was so brave, that during the Lord's crucifixion, when almost all of the apostles left Him, she stood at the foot of the cross with the Mother of God and St. John. And she kept on believing in the Lord after He died, when everyone was so very sad and confused. Perhaps that is why He chose her to be the first to see Him after He rose from the dead—because she had never stopped believing!

This is how it happened. Like almost everyone in Israel, St. Mary Magdalene was Jewish, and after Jewish people died, their friends and relatives would go to their tombs with oils and spices to anoint their bodies. On Sunday morning, after the Lord was buried, she went to the tomb with two of her friends, another Mary and Joanna. This took a lot of courage because there were Roman soldiers guarding the cave where the Lord's body lay. They had orders to not let anyone go in, and they had long sharp swords that they didn't mind using at all if people didn't do as they said.

There were not only soldiers with swords, but there was also a huge stone rolled in front of the tomb. Mary Magdalene and the other women didn't know how they could make the soldiers let them in, nor did they know how they would roll the heavy stone away. The one thing they did know was that they loved the Lord, and so they went to the tomb even though they were afraid. Have you ever loved someone so much that you wanted to do something for him that seemed impossible? If you have, then you will know how Mary and her friends felt.

Do you remember what happened next? If you are very little you might not know, but if you are bigger, you surely remember from Pascha. When they got to the tomb, they found the guards asleep, with their swords lying beside them on the grass, and the stone already rolled away! Then, as they came closer, they saw two shining angels sitting by the tomb, who said, "Why do you look for Him among the dead? He is risen!"

The women were so surprised that they ran back to tell the apostles. The apostles didn't believe them at first, but Peter and John ran to the tomb, anyway. They saw for themselves that it was empty—only the Lord's grave clothes were left lying there. The apostles went back home sadly, thinking that someone had stolen the Lord's body, but Mary stayed behind in the garden. She thought about how much she missed the Lord, and then she became so sad that she began to weep. Suddenly, a man came to her and said, "Woman, why are you weeping? Who are you searching for?" She thought he was the gardener and replied, "Sir, if you have carried him away, please tell me where you have put him, and I will take him away." But it wasn't a gardener, it was Jesus Himself. He was in his resurrected body, which was different than his earthly body, and she didn't know Him. Then, He looked at her and said, "Mary!" When she heard Him call her name, she knew it was the Lord, and she cried, "Master!" He said, "Don't touch me. I have not yet ascended to my Father. Go back to my brothers and tell them that I am going to Him who is My Father and your Father, who is My God and your God." Later, everyone saw Him, but Mary was the first.

Now, I will tell you about this picture. After the Lord ascended to heaven, Saint Mary wanted to tell everyone about His life, and how He is the Saviour of the world. She traveled to many lands to spread the gospel, and now she is called "Equal to the Apostles." According to Church tradition, she even walked to Rome, where she went to call on the Roman Emperor in his palace. In the picture you can see Saint Mary, and Caesar sitting on his throne. The Roman soldier behind him is just like the ones who were guarding Jesus' tomb.

Saint Mary Magdalene

In those days, you had to bring Caesar a gift when you went to talk to him. It was not easy to get to talk to the ruler of the whole Roman Empire, so if you were allowed to see him, you brought the very nicest present you could. People from rich families gave wonderful gifts—fantastic jewels from far-off kingdoms, or togas sewn with golden thread, or magnificent war horses. People who were less wealthy gave things like silver goblets, or bottles of fine wine. Even the poor, who had nothing else, gave an egg. Now, Saint Mary Magdalene was from a wealthy family, so Caesar was very surprised when he saw that his gift was just a plain old egg. What he didn't know was that Saint Mary had given away all of her possessions to help the Lord and His Apostles. She explained to Caesar that she was no longer rich, but that she had found a different kind of wealth in Jesus Christ. She told him about the Lord being the Son of God, and that, just as an egg holds new life, so the tomb held Jesus, Who rose from the dead and gives life to the world. Unfortunately, earthly rulers are sometimes narrow-minded, and don't believe in much beside themselves. Caesar was like this. He pointed to the egg and said, "I would sooner believe that this egg is red than that a man rose from the dead!" (The egg, of course was white, and what he meant was that he didn't believe in Christ's resurrection at all.) But as he was speaking, the egg in Mary's outstretched hand turned red before his very eyes! I'm sorry to say that even though God gave him this wonderful sign, Caesar still didn't believe, but as we all know, that didn't stop the truth of the gospel from being spread to the ends of the earth.

So, that is why we give red eggs to each other at Pascha—to celebrate the heavenly life given to us by the Lord when He rose from the dead. Saint Mary was the first to see the Lord after His resurrection, and she also gave the first Paschal egg.

After she went to Rome, Saint Mary traveled to many other places—some say even as far as France. She ended her days as a hermit in a cave, praying to the Lord, Whom she loved more than life itself, and Who she had believed in from the beginning.

Holy Saint Mary Magdalene, pray to God for us!

Saint Mary of Egypt

This is a true story about a holy woman who lived alone in a desert, the good hermit who helped her, and a powerful lion. (The lion comes in at the end.)

As her name tells us, Saint Mary was from Egypt, but the most interesting part of her life was spent in the Holy Land, where our Lord had lived. Mary had a good home, but when she got older she left her family who loved her, and completely forgot about God. She didn't pray, she wouldn't work, and she didn't do kind things for other people. She only wanted to go to wild parties and please herself. Soon she began to use her body to lead young men astray, and because she was doing things that God doesn't allow (because He knows they aren't good for us), she began to feel a little crazy.

But God never gives up trying to make us happy and at peace with Him, and one day Mary saw many people running towards the harbor where the ships were docked. She asked where they were going and they told her that they were sailing to the Holy Land for the Feast of the Exaltation of the Cross, at the Holy Sepulchre. (You remember, don't you, that the Holy Sepulchre is the most important church in the world because it is built on the place where Our Lord was crucified and rose from the dead.) Mary wasn't interested in the church feast, but she did think that there might be music and dancing and drinking on the ship. She could also see that there were many young men to tempt, so she decided to go along. Although the pilgrims were travelling to the Holy Land, Mary's journey was anything but holy. By the time the ship docked, her soul was groaning under the weight of her sins.

When the pilgrims landed, Mary traveled with them to Jerusalem. The city was full of people who had gathered for the feast, and the most crowded place of all was the courtyard leading to the Holy Sepulchre. Everyone wanted to get into the church to see the True Cross, and you never saw anything like the pushing and shoving that was going on. Mary pushed too—she had sharp elbows and knew how to use them—and very soon, she was near the door. She could already feel the cool air of the church on her face. The fragrant incense smelled wonderful, and she could see the little lamps twinkling like hundreds of stars above the Holy Sepulchre, but just as she was about to step over the threshold, she felt herself stuck fast. She couldn't get through the door! At first she thought that there were too many people crowding in at once, so she backed up and pushed her way to the front again. She knew she could do it this time! But once again, she found herself stopped. It was as if an invisible band of soldiers barred the door. Everyone was going in and out easily, except Mary. She tried again and again until she was exhausted, and finally sat down in the courtyard to rest, wondering "What can be wrong?" Then suddenly, she knew! She couldn't enter the church because she had forgotten God. Her sins were so heavy that she didn't even have enough grace left in her soul to get through the door!

At that moment, Mary turned to the Lord. She knew that she wanted to be inside the Holy Sepulchre more than anything in the world, but she couldn't do it by herself. Suddenly, she saw an icon of the Mother of God over the church door, and Mary began to beg the Holy Virgin to allow her to enter. She prayed for a long time, asking for forgiveness and promising to change her ways, if only she would be allowed in. Then—not because she had done anything good, but only because she had promised to try—she found that she was able to pass through the door easily! Her soul was filled with such joy that she felt as if she had wings. She threw herself down and kissed the floor of the church, and then, with the other pilgrims, she knelt and prayed for a long time before the life-giving Cross.

When Mary left the church, she went again to icon of the Mother of God and prayed, "O loving Lady, lead me by the hand along the path of repentance!" Suddenly she heard a voice from on high, "If you cross the Jordan, you will find glorious rest!" Mary knew that it was the Mother of God herself who was speaking to her, and she cried aloud, "O Lady, Lady, do not forsake me!" She left Jerusalem and quickly made her way to the Church of Saint John the Forerunner, by the River

Jordan, where she received Holy Communion. On the river bank she found a small boat, and getting in, she crossed over the Jordan to begin her new life in the desert.

If you have ever been to a desert you will know that it is very hot and rocky. There aren't any trees to shade you in the summer, only low scratchy bushes, and if you are fortunate, maybe a cave or two. In Mary's desert there weren't any other people, only wild animals, but the Mother of God knew all about them and protected her. In fact, she protected her so well that Mary never saw one of them, all the time she lived there.

Now, we all get a little wild sometimes when we are young, and end up making messes. I'm sure you know what I'm talking about when I say that cleaning up can be really difficult. After you feel like you've been scrubbing for hours you look around and see that you still aren't done, and you begin to think that maybe the fun you had wasn't worth the trouble it caused. Well, cleaning souls is the same, and Saint Mary had to spend not just a few hours, but many years, scrubbing hers. God had forgiven her, of course, the very first time she asked, but she had to work hard at changing her thoughts and her feelings to make sure she didn't forget Him again. It wasn't easy living in the desert, and she didn't have nice things to eat. She had taken only three little loaves of bread with her, and after they ran out she had to live on the tiny (and not very tasty) plants that grew in the desert. Her clothes became ragged, and the hot sun burnt her skin. She was lonely, too. She missed her friends, but she knew she would only get into trouble if she went back, so she stayed in the desert and prayed to the Lord and His Holy Mother to help her.

Of course, the Lord helps everyone who asks, but sometimes, as with Mary, He helps us slowly so that we learn our lesson well, and don't forget Him again. Little by little, Mary's soul came close to God, and after a long time she became not only a good woman, but a very holy one.

Now, every year, an old monk named Father Zosimas came to the desert to pray before Pascha. One spring he went further into the desert than usual and while he was praying, he saw Mary. Father Zosimas was amazed that she lived in the desert by herself, and after Mary told him her story he wanted to help her. You remember, of course, that Mary had not received Holy Communion since she had crossed the Jordan many years before, and she begged Father Zosimas to bring the Body and Blood of the Lord when he came the following year. So, he went back to his monastery, and the next spring he returned with the Holy Gifts. When he got to the river, however, he wondered how he would cross it. There was no boat, and he certainly couldn't swim carrying the Holy Mysteries.

Suddenly, he saw Mary on the other side of the river. She made the Sign of the Cross and then began to walk towards him *on top of the water*! He was astonished because this was something that the Lord Himself had done while He was on earth. It is a great miracle of God and only those who are very close to Him can do something so wonderful. When Mary reached the river bank, she knelt and prayed, and then Father Zosimas gave her Holy Communion. You can imagine how peaceful and happy that made her.

The next spring, Father Zosimas hurried into the desert to find Mary again, but she was no longer alive. God had taken her to heaven. Her body lay peacefully by the river, and she had written Father Zosimas a little note in the sand before she died. It said "Abba Zosimas, bury on this spot the body of humble Mary. Return to dust that which is dust and pray to the Lord for me...."

Father Zosimas was very sorry, of course, that he had lost his holy friend, and he knelt in the sand and wept. He wanted to bury her as she had asked, but the ground was very hard and he had nothing to dig with. He tried to make a hole with a small stick, but because he was an old man, and the sun was hot, and the work was hard, he soon became worn out. He stopped to rest, and looking up, he saw a huge lion bounding towards him out of the far desert. Father Zosimas was sure he was about to be eaten—but instead the lion ran straight to Mary's body, and bending down, licked her feet. Father Zosimas understood then that the lion had been sent by God, and said, "The Great One ordered that her body was to be buried, but

Saint Mary of Egypt

I am old and don't have the strength. Will you help me?" Even before he finished speaking, the lion began to dig with his powerful claws. Soon the grave was deep enough, and Father Zosimas gently placed Mary's body into the ground. Then he covered her with earth, and kneeling down, thanked God for her holy life. When Father Zosimas finished praying, the lion turned, and swishing his tail, ran back into the desert. Father Zosimas returned to his monastery and told the monks everything that had happened. Later, a Patriarch named Sophronios wrote it all down, and that is why we know all about Saint Mary. Even today, if you go to the Holy Sepulchre in Jerusalem, you can see the door she tried to enter, and you can pray before a piece of the Lord's Cross, the same Cross that Saint Mary saw.

In the picture you can see Father Zosimas giving Saint Mary Holy Communion. Father Zosimas also became a saint, but that was later, which is why he doesn't have a halo here. Saint Mary is wearing one of Father Zosimas' cloaks because her own clothes wore out in the desert. Behind her is the River Jordan, which she walked across, and on the far shore is the lion. I've always wondered if this lion was a grandson of Saint Gerasim's lion—the one who became Saint Gerasim's friend after he pulled a thorn out of its paw. What do you think?

Holy Saint Mary of Egypt, pray to God for us!

Saint Moses the Black

If you turn to the picture on the next page, I think you will wonder what is happening. The monk's name is Saint Moses the Black, and he was from Africa. That is why we call him Saint Moses the Black, so that we know that it is him and not the Holy Prophet Moses we are talking about. You can see that he lived in Africa, because of the palm leaves on the roof of his hut. Did you notice the halo around his head? That means that a person is so close to God, that God's own light shines from him.

Before he became a monk, Saint Moses was a robber. He was not only a robber; he was the chief of the most terrible band of cutthroats anywhere. He was very tall and strong, and if people didn't give him what he asked for, he and his seventy robbers just took it. Once, he set out to kill an unfortunate shepherd who had made him angry. When the shepherd heard that the robber chief was coming, he was so frightened that he took his flock of sheep and escaped to the other side of the Nile River. Soon the savage chief arrived, his sword drawn and ready to kill. When he saw the shepherd on the opposite shore, he didn't even wait for a boat, but ran to the river bank, wrapped his tunic around his head, put his great sword between his teeth, and swam straight across the crocodile-infested river. The poor shepherd saw him coming, and quickly buried himself in the sand. The robber searched for a long time, and when he couldn't find the shepherd, he was so mad that he killed the man's two best rams instead. He tied the dead sheep together and then swam back through the crocodiles, dragging the wooly corpses behind him. When he reached the shore, he roasted the rams over a blazing fire and ate until he almost burst. Later, he went to the village and sold the rest of the meat and the skins for wine to take back to his men. They stayed up all night drinking and singing rowdy songs about what terrible bandits they were. You can see for yourself that this isn't the way to do things.

Saint Moses the Black

This is only the beginning of the story, however, because after a while the robber chief met a monk who wasn't a bit afraid of him, and told him to his face that even though he was the most powerful man in the desert, God was stronger still. This ferocious robber chief, who had terrorized all of Egypt, was actually as weak as a baby in his soul because he had never tried to do anything good! He had no spiritual muscles. When he heard what the monk said, he didn't like it one bit, and decided that he would have to repent and become a monk himself. You see, many bad people have a small spark of good left in them, and if God can get hold of it, He can fan it into a very great blaze. What God wanted was for the robber chief to become a spiritual warrior and fight against the devil, which is much harder than fighting men.

One of the first things that the robber chief did after becoming a monk was to go back and get his seventy men to come and be Christians too. They had to work hard for a while, giving back the things they had stolen, and asking forgiveness from people they had hurt, but they were glad afterwards when their consciences stopped bothering them.

Although he knew that Our Lord Jesus Christ had forgiven him, Moses (that was the robber chief's name after he was baptized) always tried to remember his past sins, so that he wouldn't commit them again. We know he did remember them, because once, after he had become a desert father, some of the other monks wanted him to come and help them punish a brother who had done something wrong. When St. Moses came to the church, he had a big basket of sand on his shoulder. The monks said, "Father Moses, what are you doing with that sand?" Father Moses said, "You want me to punish this brother for his small fault, when I have as many sins as the grains of sand in this basket!" They understood then that he was telling them to have mercy and forgive their brother, so they did.

But the picture shows a different time, after Father Moses had lived as a monk for many years. One day some thieves came to his hut in order to kill him and take his things. These particular thieves were new in Egypt and didn't know that monks don't have anything worth stealing. They also didn't know that Father Moses had been a famous robber chief. Father Moses had already been fasting for seven days when they showed up, but he was still very strong, and he knew exactly what to do with them. He tied them up very tightly with ropes, lifted them onto his back as easily as if they were made of straw, and took them to the Abbot.

You can imagine how astonished and foolish the robbers felt at being hauled off like so many sacks of potatoes. They probably wished they hadn't gotten out of bed that morning. I'm sure they expected to be punished, but Saint Moses and the Abbot only talked to them about how much more profitable it would be to work for heavenly treasure than to steal. These thieves must have had good sparks in their hearts too, because they all agreed to become monks and spent the rest of their lives serving God and helping their neighbors.

Later, when Saint Moses was old and already very holy, ferocious barbarians invaded the desert, burning down towns and villages and killing everyone in their path. Although Saint Moses was still very strong and could easily have fought them off, he felt so bad about the people he had slain when he was a robber that he and some of his monks just let the barbarians kill them without a fight. You see, Saint Moses was a very just man, and although he knew that the Lord had forgiven him, he thought that he should allow someone to take his life because he had taken so many other lives. (Kind of like giving back something that's stolen.) It was a very noble thing to do, and after Saint Moses and his brothers died, a monk who was hiding nearby saw golden crowns descend upon them from heaven. God had counted them as martyrs!

Holy Saint Moses, pray to God for us!

Saint Nicholas the Wonderworker

Have any children ever told you there was no Santa Claus? If they did, they were wrong. There *is* a Santa Claus, a real one, and he did give presents. He was the bishop of Myra, and was so close to God that he worked miracles while he was still on earth. We know him as Saint Nicholas, and if you are in trouble you only have to ask, and he will help you. The Italians call him "Sant Nikolas," but when they came to America, the English-speaking people thought they were saying "Santa Claus." (Do you hear how the two names sound alike— "Sant Nikolas" and "Santa Claus"?) Later they forgot about his being a bishop, and only remembered the presents. The bishop part was important, though, because Saint Nicholas was a man of God. When you get a little older you will learn about how he ruled the church, but because you are still young I think you would rather hear about the presents, so that is what I am going to tell you.

There was once a rich merchant who had three beautiful daughters. One day, however, he lost all his money, and he and his daughters became so poor that they didn't have enough to eat. Their nice clothes began to wear out, and because they couldn't buy new ones, they suffered from the cold. The merchant was very worried, and he began to think that it would be better to sell his daughters to wicked men rather than let them starve. But our Lord Jesus Christ, who sees everything and knows all our thoughts, knew what was in this man's heart, and decided to help the girls through His servant, Nicholas. At that time, Nicholas was still a young priest, but he was so close to God that he easily understood what God wanted him to do. Late one night, when everyone was asleep, Father Nicholas went to the merchant's house and threw a bag of gold through the window. When the merchant awoke in the morning and saw the gold lying on the floor, he was overjoyed. He bought food for his children and gave his oldest daughter a dowry so that she could marry. (In those days girls had to bring a dowry—gifts of money or furniture, or land, or farm animals with them when they married, to help set up housekeeping.)

But when the gold was gone and the man still had two daughters left to feed and give dowries to, he began to think again about selling them. Father Nicholas knew this, and because he was pleased that the man had used the first bag of gold in such a good way, he came secretly and threw another bag through the window. You can imagine how the merchant's eyes popped out when he woke up and saw the second bag of gold. Now he was able to buy warm clothes and give his second daughter in marriage.

The merchant had only his youngest daughter left, and he thought, "Maybe this good person will throw another bag of gold through the window for my third daughter, and if I stay awake, I will see who it is." So, night after night, he forced himself to stay up. You know how hard it is to stay awake for even a few hours when you are tired. Your eyelids feel like stones, and you have to keep pinching yourself hard not to fall off your chair. But somehow the merchant managed. He didn't allow himself to sleep even a wink until the morning sun peeped through the window of his tiny cottage. Finally, one night when there was no moon but the sky was full of stars, he heard someone come quietly to his window. The merchant sat as still as a statue, not even daring to breathe, and just when he thought he would burst, the third bag of gold came flying through the air and landed at his feet!

The merchant jumped up and ran out into the street, where he found Father Nicholas slipping away into the darkness. He fell on his knees before the young priest, thanking him for his kindness, but Father Nicholas made him promise not to tell anyone about the gold. (You see, the young priest cared more for the honor of God than the honor of men.) Then, Father Nicholas spoke to the merchant about how he needed to put his trust in God when he was in trouble, rather than thinking up silly plans like selling his children. The merchant promised have more faith, for even he could see that it was God Who was watching over him.

Saint Nicholas the Wonderworker

So that is how Saint Nicholas came to be known for giving presents. Christians still pray to him, and he helps with things like food and clothes, and getting innocent people out of prison, and saving you if you are on a stormy sea and your boat is about to sink. He especially watches over people who are traveling and those who don't have anyone to care for them—like women whose husbands have died, or children who don't have a mother or father. If we ask, he will also pray to God for spiritual gifts for us, like faith and love and pure hearts, so that we can be as close to God as he is.

In the picture Saint Nicholas is throwing the gold through the window. There are really three girls, but the window is so tiny you can only see two of them. Their father is asleep on the other side of the room, and you can't see him at all.

Holy Saint Nicholas, pray to God for us!

Saint Nina of Georgia

Most of us are able to choose how we will serve God—whether we will be married and have a family, or be a monk or a nun, or maybe a teacher, a carpenter, or an artist. Some people, however, are given special things to do by God, and Saint Nina was one of these. When she was a young girl, she was chosen by the Mother of God to enlighten the land of Georgia (or Iberia, as it was called in those days.) You see, there is a very old story that when the Mother of God was still on earth, she wanted to go with the Twelve Apostles to preach the gospel. They drew lots to see where they should go, and the Mother of God chose the land of Iberia. She began to prepare for her journey, but one day the Archangel Gabriel appeared to her and told her that God did not want her to go to Georgia, that she was to remain in the Holy Land. So she stayed in Jerusalem until the Lord took her to heaven, but she never forgot the people of Iberia who had not yet learned about her Divine Son and the promise of the Holy Gospel.

Three hundred years later, when Emperor Constantine and his mother, Saint Helen, ruled the Roman Empire, the Mother of God came to Nina one night and said, "Depart into the land of the north and preach the gospel of my Son, and I will guide you and protect you." (You see, she was choosing Nina to go in her place to Iberia.) But Nina was frightened by these words and said, "Heavenly Queen, how am I to do this, for I am a worthless and ignorant woman." Then the Most Holy Virgin stretched out her hand and plucked a vine-branch that grew close to Nina's bed. She made it into a cross, and gave it to Nina saying, "Let this cross be your protection. By its power you will overcome all your foes and preach your message. I will be with you and will never leave you." When Nina awoke she found in her hand the very cross that had been fashioned by the Mother of God!

Nina set off, and she traveled for many weeks. She prayed very hard along the way, for her road lay through high mountains infested by terrible bandits and wild bears and wolves. After many adventures, she arrived in Iberia, where she went to the city of the great King Mirian. There, she found some kind Jewish people to stay with, who taught her the Iberian language and the ways of the people.

One day a great procession of Iberians, including King Mirian and Queen Nana, set out from the palace in splendid dress and with great ceremony to visit the high temple, where they worshipped an idol called Armazi. Nina followed them, and watched from afar as the people adored this false god. The pagan priests had made an image of him out of copper, in the form of a man. The idol was clothed in golden armor, and his eyes were made from emeralds and beryl stones. At his side was a sword, which flashed like lightning. On the idol's right and left were two other lifeless gods named Gaim and Gatsi, crafted of gold and silver.

Nina was sad when she saw the people pouring their love into these dead idols, instead of worshipping their Creator, and she began to weep and pray, "O God, throw down these false idols, Thine enemies, and through Thy great mercy, make these people wise, so that the whole land will worship Thee as the true God, through the power of Thy Son Jesus Christ...."

As soon as she uttered her prayer, the Lord sent strong winds and rain out of the west. Huge black clouds gathered over the mountain top, and thunder began to roll across the sky like a giant war drum. The people were terribly frightened and they all began to run down the mountain side, back to the town. As soon as they had gone, the Lord unloosed his wrath and huge rocks of hail fell onto the pagan temple, crushing the building and its false idols.

Nina went back to the city, and near its walls she found a bramble bush growing in the shape of a small tent, which she decided to make her home. She didn't have any icons, so she made a cross of vine-shoots (like the one the Mother of God had made for her) and tied it with a strand of her hair. Then she began to pray night and day. Soon the townspeople understood that she was a holy woman, and they brought many sick folk to her, that God might heal them through her prayers.

Saint Nina of Georgia

One day Queen Nana fell ill with a painful disease. The royal physicians tried all of their medicines and remedies, but nothing helped. At last, when the doctors had given up hope, the Queen's friends told her about Nina, and how she healed the sick. Soon, the people of the city saw a strange sight: the Queen of all Iberia was carried to the humble little bush-house and laid on Nina's prayer rug. Nina prayed to the Lord for a long time, and then, taking her vine-branch cross, she touched it to the Queen's head, feet and shoulders, in the Sign of the Cross. Queen Nana rose up in perfect health. Not only was her body made well, but her soul was also healed, for now she knew in her heart that Jesus Christ was the true God.

When the Queen arrived home, King Mirian was very surprised and wanted to know how she had gotten well so quickly. When she told him, he was amazed. It took him a little longer to see that Christianity is the true faith, but when he finally did, he came to visit Nina. Kneeling down in her little bush-house, he, too, confessed that Christ is the Son of God. Then King Mirian wrote a letter to Emperor Constantine telling him that because of Nina's preaching the whole land of Iberia wanted to be Christian. He asked the Emperor to send priests to baptize the people and give them Holy Communion. Nina also wrote a letter to Saint Helen, the Emperor's mother, telling her how God had thrown down the idols and converted the people's hearts. Emperor Constantine was very glad to hear that the Iberians wanted to be baptized, and he sent many priests to help. He also sent wonderful gifts: beautiful icons, shining candlesticks, and golden chalices for the churches. King Mirian and Queen Nana became great missionaries themselves, but they always honored Saint Nina, whom they called "the mother of our country." Saint Nina spent the rest of her life traveling throughout Georgia, teaching the good news of Our Lord Jesus Christ and preparing the people for baptism.

What Saint Nina did was so wonderful that now we call her "Equal to the Apostles." In the picture you can see her praying for the people, and in the distance, the false idols are tumbling into a heap at the bottom of the mountain, just where they belong.

Holy Saint Nina, pray to God for us!

Great Martyr and Healer Panteleimon

Do you know who Saint Panteleimon is? In his icon, he always holds a little box. Can you guess what is in it? Before Saint Panteleimon was a martyr, that is, before he died for Christ, he was a doctor. But he wasn't like any doctor you've ever met, and I think after you've heard his story you will agree with me.

Saint Panteleimon was born in the city of Nicomedia. His father, Eustogius, was a wealthy pagan and his mother, Euboula, was a Christian. They named their son "Pantoleon," which means, "in everything a lion." As you can see, they expected him to grow into a great man. Unfortunately, Euboula died when Pantoleon was still young, and his pagan father taught the young boy to worship the Roman gods.

Pantoleon was very bright, and because his father was a wealthy and important man, the youth was trained as a doctor at the palace of Emperor Maximian. The Emperor soon noticed him and told Pantoleon's teachers to hurry with his education so that he could be the Emperor's own physician. Although Emperor Maximian liked Pantoleon, in other ways he was not a good or just ruler. The Emperor especially hated Christians and had ordered his soldiers to kill any Christians they found.

Every night on his way home from the palace, Pantoleon passed a house where an old Christian priest named Hermolaus lived secretly with a few of his disciples. They lived in hiding so that Maximian's soldiers would not find them, but Father Hermolaus often saw Pantoleon pass by. The old priest knew that Pantoleon was chosen by God, and one day, he invited him to come in for a talk. Pantoleon told the priest of his past, of his mother's Christianity and his father's paganism, and of his desire to become a doctor. In return, Father Hermolaus told the boy of the Divine Physician who surpasses all earthly physicians, and who can heal both body and soul—the Lord Jesus Christ.

Pantoleon visited Father Hermolaus often, but he still wasn't sure that he believed in the Christian God. One day, on his way home from the palace, he found the body of a dead child who had been bitten by a snake. The snake was also dead, and it lay in the road beside the boy. Pantoleon felt so sorry that he decided the time had come to test the promises of Father Hermolaus. He dropped to his knees beside the dead child and prayed, "Lord Jesus Christ, even though I am unworthy to call upon Thee, if Thou dost wish me to become Thy servant, show Thy power, that in Thy Name, this child may be healed." The boy opened his eyes as if he had only been asleep, jumped up, and ran home crying. Pantoleon was amazed and he blessed and glorified the Christian God. Then he ran to the priest's house, and telling Father Hermolaus what had happened, begged to be baptized. When he heard Pantoleon's story, Father Hermolaus went with him to look at the snake and at the place where the boy had been brought back to life by the power of Christ. Then, he baptized Pantoleon and gave him Holy Communion.

Not long after, a blind man who had spent all of his money on doctors who hadn't been able to help him, came to Pantoleon and begged him to restore his sight. Pantoleon's father, Eustogius, didn't want him to try, because the best doctors in the city hadn't been able to help, and Pantoleon wasn't even a doctor yet. But Pantoleon told his father it would be all right, and quietly placing his hands over the man's eyes, called on the Lord to give him back his sight. At that very moment the man began to see. He and Eustogius were so amazed by the power of Christ that they, too, were baptized. Afterwards Pantoleon and his father smashed all the Roman idols in their home to bits.

Eustogius soon became ill and died. Pantoleon, who was now very wealthy, gave his family's slaves their freedom and distributed his riches among the city's widows and orphans. He visited prisoners to make sure they had enough food and clothes, and healed them when they were sick. Anyone who asked received his help. He wouldn't take any money because he knew that healing is from God, and he told those who wanted to pay to give the money to the poor instead. Everyone grew to love Pantoleon—everyone, that is, except the other physicians, who

Saint Panteleimon

were so jealous of the young doctor that they went to the Emperor and complained that Pantoleon was turning the people into Christians.

The Emperor was very upset because he liked Pantoleon and wanted him to be his own physician, but it was against the law for anyone to be a Christian. When the young man was brought before the Emperor, Maximian questioned him gently, asking Pantoleon if it was true that he didn't believe in the pagan gods. Instead of answering him, Pantoleon suggested that he have a contest of healing with the temple priests, to see who could cure a paralyzed beggar. Everyone knew this man, who for many years had lain by the palace gates, asking the passersby for help. The Emperor agreed, and after the beggar was brought in, the pagan priests began to call upon their gods. They chanted spells and made sacrifices, but because they were praying to dumb idols, there was no answer. Finally, they gave up, and it was Pantoleon's turn. Pantoleon went up to the paralyzed man, called upon the name of Jesus Christ, and the man rose up from his bed, completely healed.

Of course, the pagan priests were very angry and they told the Emperor that Pantoleon had won the contest by magic, and that if the Emperor didn't kill him, the Roman gods would be angry and destroy the palace. Maximian was very frightened. He had believed in these false gods all his life, and he told Pantoleon that he must sacrifice to the idols or be put to death. The young man answered, "Everyone who has died for Christ has not perished but has found eternal life.... If I do not die for Christ, life shall be meaningless. I count my death as gain."

Maximian had Pantoleon harshly tortured to make him bow down to the idols, but each time the Lord saved him. First, he was hung up and his body was scraped with iron hooks and burnt with candles, but the hands of the soldiers soon weakened as if they were paralyzed. Then he was thrown into a tub of red-hot tin, but the tin cooled as soon as the Saint touched it. Next, Pantoleon was cast into the depths of the sea with a stone tied around his neck, but the Lord miraculously upheld him on the water and the stone floated like a leaf. Finally he was put into the arena to be eaten by wild beasts, but they only crowded around him, eager to lick his feet and receive his blessing. When he heard this, Emperor Maximian was beside himself with rage and fear, and ordered that Pantoleon be beheaded.

Pantoleon was taken outside the city and tied to an olive tree, but when the soldier tried to strike his head off with the sword, the iron bent like wax because the martyr had not yet finished saying his prayers. Seeing this, the soldiers all cried out, "Great is the God of the Christians!" and they fell at the Saint's feet, begging his forgiveness. Then, as Pantoleon prayed, a voice was heard from heaven declaring that his name was now Panteleimon, which means "the all-merciful one." The soldiers did not want to kill him, but Saint Panteleimon said that it was the will of Christ and that they must be obedient. Weeping, they struck off his head, and from his body there flowed milk instead of blood. At that moment, the olive tree to which the martyr was tied burst into fruit. The Emperor was so angry that he ordered the soldiers to chop up the olive tree into little pieces and burn it with the Saint's body. Even after death, however, the Lord protected his Saint, and when the fire died down, everyone saw that his body wasn't a bit burnt. Later, some of Saint Panteleimon's Christian servants buried his relics and wrote down his story.

Orthodox Christians still come to Saint Panteleimon when they are ill, and there are many people who have been healed by his warm prayers before the Lord. Can you guess what he is holding in the box now? Yes, it's medicine, of course! And even if you can't read the names of the saints on their icons, you can always tell Saint Panteleimon because he is holding his medicine box, awaiting the prayer of anyone who needs his help.

Holy Saint Panteleimon, pray to God for us!

Saint Philothei

Saint Philothei of Athens

About five hundred years ago, there was a young woman named Philothei who lived in Athens, Greece. This wasn't so long ago that people still worshipped pagan idols—in Greece everyone was already Christian. Nevertheless, it was a difficult time for Christians because Turkish Moslems had conquered the country and many young people had been taken from their families. Young men were sometimes forced to become Moslem soldiers, and young women who had been captured by pirates were sold as slaves.

Philothei came from a wealthy Christian family, and after her mother and father died she used the money they had left her to build hospitals and care for orphans and the poor. She worked hard taking care of sick folk, and sometimes God even healed them through her prayers. One day Saint Andrew the Apostle appeared to her from heaven and told her that God wanted her to build a church and a monastery. So she did. She became the first abbess of the monastery, and her family's servants—who loved her so much they didn't want to leave her—became the first nuns.

Long before Christians were helping American slaves escape to freedom, Philothei was doing the very same thing in Athens. When runaway Christian slaves came to her, she would hide them in her monastery or in a little cave where she sometimes went to pray. (The cave is still in Athens, and you can see it if you go there.) Later, when no one was watching, she would send the runaways down to the harbor where there was a ship waiting to take them to safety. Once they escaped, they could return to their homes.

Of course, if you were a runaway slave, the dangerous part was getting to the ship without anyone seeing you. You had to wait until sunset, and then walk swiftly and quietly through the dark, narrow streets of the town and across the hills to the harbor. The harbor was far away, and when there was no moon, you had to walk very carefully so that you didn't stumble on the rocky road or step on a snake. If you've ever walked on a road where you had to be especially watchful, you will remember how tired you felt from paying attention to every single step. An escaped slave couldn't have a lantern either, because if anyone saw you they would take you straight back to your master. If you heard someone coming on the road you would have to slip off into the bushes and not let yourself move or cough or sneeze. Your heart would pound so loudly in your chest that you were sure the passerby could hear it, and you would just close your eyes and pray until he went on. Finally, with the help of the Lord and His saints, you reached the harbor where the waiting sailors would row you to the ship, put up the sails, and carry you to freedom.

Once, when she was young, Philothei was caught helping Christian slaves escape and was almost put to death. As she grew older, though, she became very clever and even though the Turks knew that she was freeing their slaves, they couldn't catch her. Because they couldn't catch her, they couldn't put her in prison. One night, a group of Turkish men came to Philothei's monastery, tied her to a pillar, and beat her to make her stop helping the slaves. She was already old by this time, and she died a few weeks later. Now the Church calls her Saint Philothei and we say that she was a martyr because she died helping other Christians. We still ask her to pray for orphans, the poor and sick, and those who are suffering under Moslem rule. She is the heavenly protector of the people of Athens, but even if we don't live there we can ask her to help us to be as kind and brave and clever as she was in doing God's work.

In the picture Saint Philothei is helping the Christian slave girls escape to the ship that is waiting to take them to freedom.

Holy Saint Philothei, pray to God for us!

Saint Seraphim of Sarov

Is there an Orthodox child anywhere who does not know the name of this wonderful Saint? Of course not. It's simply impossible. This is Saint Seraphim of Sarov, the "Batiushka of All-Russia"—the father of the Russian land! I think you will agree with me when I say that in an Orthodox country like Russia, with its thousands and thousands of holy saints, that is a remarkable title!

Saint Seraphim wasn't always a saint, of course. He spent his boyhood growing up in a Russian town, and his baptismal name was Prochorus. Although Prochorus didn't become a monk until later, he was always close to God, and even when he was young, miracles happened to him. Once, when he was seven years old he climbed with his mother to the very top of a high bell tower. Like all boys, he wanted to lean over the edge to see as far as he could. The countryside with all its villages and churches and streams and little specks of cows lay like a carpet at his feet, and he leaned out farther and farther until suddenly he fell headlong off of the edge of the tower! His horrified mother rushed down the steps, thinking that he was surely dead, but when she reached the ground, she was amazed to find him standing on his feet, without a scratch, as if he had been caught by angels!

A few years later, Saint Seraphim became a monk. He knew how powerful prayer was, so he decided to pray with all his strength. For many years he lived with his brother monks in the monastery, but later he went to stay in a small cabin he had built for himself in the woods so that he could pray all the time. The thing about prayer is that the more you pray, the more you want to pray, and Saint Seraphim once prayed kneeling on a rock for a thousand days and nights! I think he probably got off once in a while to eat and sleep, but most of the time, he just prayed. If you want to see how difficult this is, try kneeling and praying on a rock for just a little while.

So, you might ask, what did Saint Seraphim accomplish by kneeling on this rock? The answer is very simple. He received the greatest gift of all, the Holy Spirit! His soul became so pure that the Holy Spirit came to live in his heart, and he was full of love—love for God, for his neighbors, and for all of creation. He was so full of God's love that a wild bear came to eat out of his hand. He was like Adam in Paradise before the Fall, and even the beasts of the forest trusted him. You see, animals haven't completely forgotten Paradise (as have some people), and they still recognize real goodness.

After he became filled with the Holy Spirit, Saint Seraphim helped many people who came to him with their sicknesses and sorrows. He would teach them how to pray and how to love God. When people came and asked him how they could help their neighbors he replied, "Acquire the spirit of peace, and thousands around you will be saved." What he meant was that when you have God's peace in your heart, everyone will see it and want to have it for themselves. Once, one of Saint Seraphim's friends saw him shining as brightly as the sun, and putting out such a heavenly warmth that, although they were sitting on a log in the snow, they weren't a bit cold!

Saint Seraphim especially loved children. Sometimes, when he wanted to be alone, he would hide in the tall grass so that visitors couldn't find him. But the pilgrims knew this, and they would send their children ahead, calling, "Batiushka! Batiushka!" and Saint Seraphim always came out. He had such great love that, instead of calling people by their names, he would call them "My Joy" and to everyone he would say, "Christ is Risen!"

In the picture you can see the bear eating out of Saint Seraphim's hand. The pilgrims coming to him through the woods look a little worried, but that is only because they haven't acquired the Holy Spirit yet. As soon as they do, they won't be afraid. Do you think Saint Seraphim called the bear, "My Joy" too?

Holy Saint Seraphim, pray to God for us!

Saint Seraphim of Sarov

Saint Xenia of Petersburg

Saint Xenia of Petersburg

Saint Xenia was a beautiful young Russian girl from the city of Saint Petersburg, who became a Fool-for-Christ, and this is how it happened.

When she was just old enough, Xenia married a dashing cavalry officer named Andrei, and they were very happy together. Because they were young, they loved going to balls and dinners, but one night at a party Andrei suddenly fell over dead! This was terrible for Xenia, of course. Andrei had not even had time to go to Confession or receive Holy Communion before he died, and she was dreadfully worried about his soul. After Andrei was buried, Xenia left Saint Petersburg for a long time and some people think she even went to a monastery. I don't know about that, but I do know that when she came back she gave away everything she had—her house, her money and her beautiful clothes. Instead of her own things, she wore Andrei's old army jacket and told everyone to call her by his name. She went all over the city doing good for people in his name, so that if his soul was suffering from sins that he hadn't repented of, her deeds and prayers would help him. Christians often give money or offer prayers for the souls of people who have died. This is called almsgiving, but it is not so common to give up your whole life for another person, which is what Xenia did. The interesting thing about doing good deeds and offering prayers for other people is that soon you become very close to God yourself, and that's what happened to Xenia. She was praying so hard for her husband that she became holy!

Many people thought that she was a little crazy, especially when she gave all her money away. But in the Orthodox Church we have a name for holy people that other people might think are crazy. We call them "Fools-for-Christ." They often aren't crazy, but just pretend to be so that they can hide their spiritual gifts. The Lord had given Xenia many spiritual gifts and she began to do odd things like walking barefoot in the snow and wearing unusual clothes so that people wouldn't think she was special. She sometimes knew what was going to happen before it happened, or if people had a problem and didn't know what God wanted them to do, she could tell them. Often just by looking at people, she knew if they were telling the truth or not.

Sometimes, when Christians do good things, they do them secretly so that only God sees. This is because the Lord said, "Let not your left hand know what your right hand is doing," and, "Do your good works in secret so that your father who sees you in secret can reward you openly." This is what this picture of Saint Xenia is about. Many years ago, when the people of Saint Petersburg were building a church in the Smolensk Cemetery, Saint Xenia used to go secretly at night and carry the heavy bricks that were needed for the next day's building to the top of the church. When the workmen came every morning, they found the hardest part of their work already finished, and they often wondered who was doing such a kind thing. Finally, two of the workmen decided to spend the night in the cemetery. They waited and waited, and when it was very dark, Saint Xenia appeared. All night long they watched her climb up and down, up and down, up and down the walls of the half-finished church with her bricks.

The church that Saint Xenia helped to build is still in the Smolensk Cemetery, and there is a tiny chapel nearby where she is buried. Pilgrims from all over Russia still come there to pray for help. During the terribly difficult years in Russia, when the churches were closed because the Communists didn't want people to worship God, pilgrims came secretly to Saint Xenia's. The door to the chapel was locked, and because they couldn't get in, they wrote their prayers to her on little scraps of paper and slipped them into the cracks in the walls. The Communists didn't like this one bit, but they soon found out that it was impossible to stop Christians from loving the Saints, or to stop the Saints from helping them!

God has healed many people of illnesses and passions through Saint Xenia's prayers. She also helps find homes and jobs. St. Xenia didn't have a home herself, and she knows how hard it is for people who need one. In the church service for her feast, we call her a "homeless wanderer," because she gave up her earthly home for heaven.

Holy Saint Xenia, pray to God for us!

Here are the feast days of the saints in this book.

Ss. Constantine and Helen	May 21
Ss. Cyprian and Justina	October 2
St. Demetrius of Thessalonica	October 26
St. Herman of Alaska	December 12, July 27
St. John the Russian	May 27
St. Mary of Egypt	April 1
St. Mary Magdalene	July 22
St. Moses the Black	August 28
St. Nicholas	December 6, May 9
St. Nina	January 14
St. Panteleimon	July 27
St. Philothei	February 19
St. Seraphim of Sarov	January 2, July 19
St. Xenia	January 24

Wondrous is God in His Saints!